This Book Belongs To:

COOKING WITH FLOWERS

COOKING
WITH
FLOWERS

Wherein An Age-Old Art Is Revived

Written by Zack Hanle

Illustrated by Donald Hendricks

SECOND PRINTING – JANUARY 1972

Printed in the United States of America. All rights reserved.
Standard Book Number 8431-0111
Library of Congress Catalogue Card Number: 74-125084

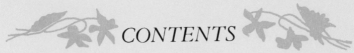

CONTENTS

To Tessie Zachariae,
the girl with the green thumb, the golden
ladle, a nose for fragrance, and a palate
for the exotic.

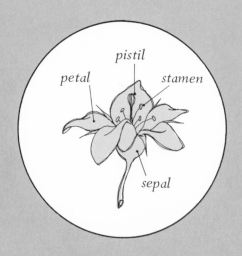

America's colonial gentlewoman cherished her centuries old, handed-down recipes for flower waters to flavor cakes, dried herblike blossoms for enhancing teas and punches, fresh posies for special salads, and fragrant leaves and blossoms for exotic tastes in jellies, jams and conserves.

Her heritage came from England where Shakespeare's audiences delighted in such rare delicacies as stewed primroses (popularly called oxlips), gillyflower cordial (carnations or pinks, we call them), and violet and rose water. In fact, the joys and delights of flower cookery date back to the beginnings of man, reaching a high peak of artistry in medieval and Elizabethan times.

Today, the use of flowers in the kitchen is almost a lost art, although scouts and hunters know the lore of wild flowers and have preserved some of the remote recipes for outdoor cooking. But as our daily lives have become more mechanized, and our food more convenient, this gentle art of cuisinery is gradually disappearing. It is hoped that this potpourri of delectables from the flower garden will help to revive it.

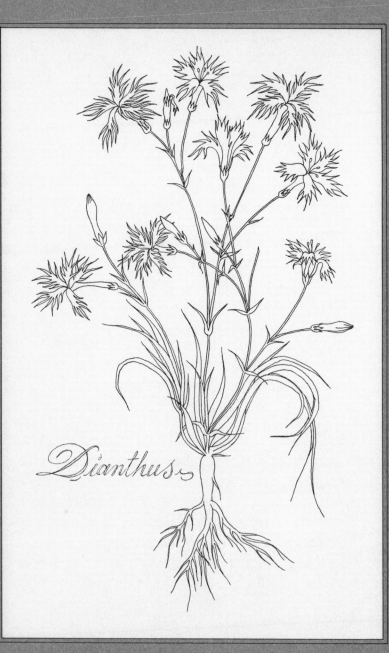

Dianthus

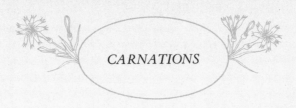

CARNATIONS

Call them gillyflowers as Shakespeare did, sops-in-wine as Chaucer referred to them, or "food for Phoebus' horses" as the philosopher Rousseau praised them — for centuries the satiny-textured flowers we often call "pinks" were highly prized for their clove-like flavor and fragrance.

Not the hothouse carnation, but the small herb Dianthus offers the spicy, colorful petals for the brews that follow.

Carnation recipes proliferated in the 17th and 18th centuries and the art of making butters, cordials, syrups, vinegars and ratafias with these piquant petals reached its peak in England around 1650. The French, too, had a way with this bit of flower cookery and the Spaniards favored both its flavor and its colorfulness.

CARNATION CORDIAL

1 pound of fresh carnation petals
1 small stick cinnamon
1 whole clove
1 pint good brandy
½ pound sugar
½ cup water

Wash and pick over carnation petals, removing all stems and sepals. Place in a one-quart container with a tight lid and add the cinnamon and clove. Pour brandy over this and seal securely, leaving sealed and stored in a cool, dark place for 4 to 6 weeks. Strain and mix with sugar syrup prepared by boiling the sugar and water for 15 minutes. Bottle and seal. Serve as a liqueur or cordial. Makes 1½ pints.

GILLYFLOWER FONDANT

½ cup red carnation petals,
    packed firmly
1 egg white
2 cups (or more) powdered
    sugar
pinch powdered cloves

Place carnation petals in a mortar and grind to a pulp
with pestle. Add sugar gradually and add egg white. Stir,
mix thoroughly, and continue adding powdered sugar
until a smooth and stiff paste is formed. Add cloves and
blend. Put paste in a pastry tube and force through to
form rosettes on a marble slab or sheet of wax paper.
Allow to dry. Makes 2-3 dozen candies.

GILLYFLOWER SAUCE

2 cups carnation petals, packed firmly
1 quart wine vinegar
1 cup granulated sugar
½ teaspoon powdered cloves
1 stick cinnamon
¼ teaspoon nutmeg

Be sure the petals are washed and their white bases snipped off. Place all ingredients in a two-quart saucepan. Bring to a boil, reduce heat and simmer for one hour. Strain. Cool. Store in refrigerator in tightly stoppered bottle. Use as a sauce for cold meats such as lamb, tongue, or ham. Keeps indefinitely.

CARNATION CUPCAKES

1 package prepared cupcake mix
1 package white icing mix
3 dozen red, pink, or striped
    Dianthus carnation flowers

Use the very smallest cupcake pans, or foil baking cups, and make three dozen tiny cupcakes. Cool and coat with white icing mix. Wash and drain the carnation flowers. Snip off at the heels (green and white bases) and place one flower in the center of each little cake. Store in refrigerator until serving time. A pretty tea accompaniment. Serves 12 or more.

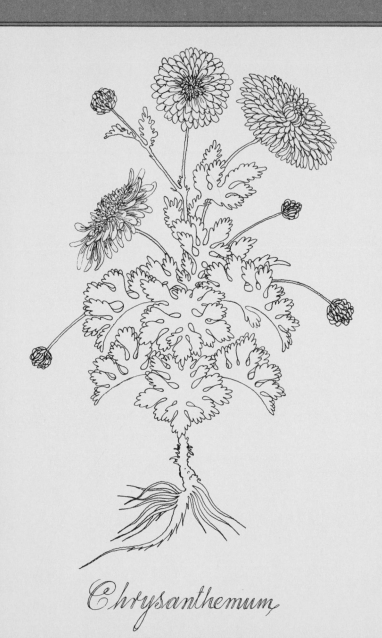

Chrysanthemum

CHRYSANTHEMUMS

The favorite flower of the Chinese philosopher Confucius was the chrysanthemum. Later, in Japan, it inspired a national holiday. Today there are thousands of varieties, all with the characteristic, pungent flavor of autumn.

The celebrated ceremonial dish known as Chrysanthemum Bowl is an enormous meal in itself, which is generally served only on special occasions in China. Its preparation is long and tedious, supervised at the festive table by the hostess herself and climaxed by the dramatic moment when the hostess plucks petals from mammoth "football" chrysanthemums and floats them on top of the steaming broth in the pot.

On the following pages, we give the long version for those who have leisure and access to the ingredients, and also a shorter contemporary recipe of our own invention which would undoubtedly cause a gentle Chinese homemaker to shudder at our Western audacity.

CHRYSANTHEMUM BOWL

8 cups chicken stock

2 teaspoons salt

1 tablespoon lard

2 giant white or yellow chrysanthemums

¼ pound bean thread (or peastarch noodles
    or fine egg noodles)

1 head of celery cabbage, shredded

1 pound fresh spinach, washed, and
    cut in diagonal strips

2 whole chicken breasts,
    sliced in very thin strips

½ pound raw shrimp, halved

½ pound chicken livers, cut very thin

1 cup small oysters, raw

½ pound pork tenderloin, sliced
    wafer-thin

1 pound white firm-fleshed fish
    (halibut, hake, cod), sliced

2 tablespoons sherry
1 tablespoon cornstarch
2 tablespoons water

Arrange all raw ingredients attractively on large platters and bring to table along with chafing dish over stove (electric, alcohol, charcoal, whichever is convenient). Chicken stock, salt and lard are brought to boil in pot at the table and guests help to add the ingredients with chopsticks or forks. Mix the sherry, cornstarch and water and add after all other ingredients have bubbled and boiled for several minutes. Finally, the petals of the chrysanthemum are plucked and floated on the savory broth just before serving. Allow guests to serve themselves just as they wish, directly from the pot. Serves 8.

CHRYSANTHEMUM CHOWDER

1 dozen medium-size
   chrysanthemum flowers
2 cans New England clam
   or fish chowder
1 lemon
1 teaspoon salt

Prepare chowder according to favorite recipe or use a good canned variety and prepare according to directions on can. Tear off the petals of the chrysanthemums and toss into a bowl of cold water to which the juice of the lemon and salt has been added. Rinse, drain, and pat blossoms between paper towels. Just before serving soup, add flower petals. Serves 4.

RISING SUN SALAD

1 dozen fresh lichee nuts
2 mangoes
2 fresh peaches
2 large bananas
4 tangerines
1 or 2 large, yellow chrysanthemums
¼ cup mayonnaise
½ cup heavy cream

Peel and slice mangoes, peaches, bananas and place in salad bowl. Peel lichee nuts and tangerines and remove tangerine segment skins. Add to bowl. Whip cream and fold into mayonnaise. Pour mixture over the fruit. Wash chrysanthemums, drain and remove petals. Scatter over the salad and serve ice cold. Serves 4.

MUM SOUP

2 cans chicken consommé
1 small can water chestnuts
2 scallions, tops only
6 sprigs parsley
1 fresh lemon, peel only
2 slices cold-boiled ham
1 large, fresh chrysanthemum
  soy sauce

Heat consommé to boiling point, but do not boil. Add sliced water chestnuts, thinly sliced green tops of scallions, shredded cold-boiled ham, and thinly slivered lemon peel. Remove petals from chrysanthemum, wash, drain and add to soup. Bring to a boil and serve at once with garnish of parsley and a dash of soy sauce in each bowl. Serves 4-6.

WESTERN CHRYSANTHEMUM BOWL

2 cans good chicken broth
1 large white or yellow chrysanthemum
1 teaspoon sherry
½ teaspoon soy sauce
6 spinach leaves, chopped fine

Bring broth to a boil and add all other ingredients with
the exception of the chrysanthemum. Pour into tureen
and bring to table. Just before serving guests, pluck
chrysanthemum petals and float them on top of the
soup. Serves 4.

Taraxacum Officinale

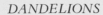

DANDELIONS

This lowly and prolific little herb is loathed by lawn-builders and adored by children, who delight in "making a wish" as they blow off the fluffy heads of the seeding flowers in the fall.

Originally a European weed, the dandelion grows in the most wretched soil. Every part of the plant is edible from root to flower head, and today, its tender inner leaves are cultivated and sold all summer long by greengrocers for use in detectable salads or as a cooked, spinach-like vegetable. Only the mature outer leaves should be discarded, simply because they are too tough and somewhat bitter.

The roots have been used for soups; the budlike whorls at the centers, as the plant forms, are an interesting vegetable when cooked and served like baby artichokes. The golden blossoms have been beloved by the British for centuries in the making of the brew called Dandelion Wine. Under cultivation, the hearts or centers of the dandelion plant, before it shoots up its flowers, may be bleached by covering. Cooked in butter, they have a flavor reminiscent of the bleached French asparagus.

DANDELION WINE

2 quarts dandelion blossoms
4 quarts water
8 whole cloves
½ teaspoon powdered ginger
1 cup orange juice
3 tablespoons lemon juice
3 tablespoons coarsely chopped
   fresh orange rind
1 tablespoon coarsely chopped
   fresh lemon peel
3 tablespoons lime juice
3 pounds granulated sugar
¼ cake compressed, dried yeast
   dissolved in
¼ cup warm water

Choose flowers from an open field rather than from a lawn and pick early in the season when the plant's leaves are still tender. Flowers that have just opened are best and just the flower heads are used. Put the washed blossoms in water with orange, lemon and lime juice. Add the citrus rinds, cloves, ginger, and sugar. Bring to boil and continue to boil for one hour. Strain through filter paper. Cool. While still warm, add yeast. Let stand overnight and pour into bottles. After three weeks, cork, and store in a cool place. Makes about 8 pints.

DANDELION SALAD

½ cup dandelion flower buds,
   unopened
1 bunch young, tender, dandelion
   leaves (about 1 pint, loosely
   packed)
2 strips. bacon
3 tablespoons vinegar and oil
   dressing

Wash dandelion flowers and leaves and pat dry between paper towels. Fry bacon strips in skillet until crisp. Remove bacon and drain on towels. Toss dandelion flowers into the bacon grease and cook till buds burst open. Drain buds. Crumble bacon into salad bowl. Add dandelion leaves and flowers. Pour dressing over all and toss lightly. Serves 4.

DANDY OMELET

1 cup dandelion flower buds
4 eggs
  pepper, salt to taste
  butter

Pick dandelion buds which are showing yellow about halfway down the bud. Remove stems, wash, and measure one cupful. Melt butter in medium-size omelet pan. Add drained and dried dandelion buds and saute just until the buds start to burst open. Pour in lightly beaten eggs. As eggs firm up on edges, lift edges and let liquid egg run under, cooking until omelet is firm all around, but still soft in center. Fold in thirds. Flip over and serve. Season to taste with salt and pepper or sprinkle some finely chopped dandelion leaves over the omelet for garnish. Serves 2-3.

Hemerocallis Aurantiaca

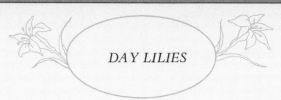

DAY LILIES

Along the summer highways the rusty-orange day lily delights the traveller. In gardens, its more refined form offers colors in every conceivable shade of yellow, orange and red, from pure lemon to lime, from buff to flame, from scarlet to mahogany.

Botanically, it's known as Hemerocallis, *meaning "beautiful for a day." Each blossom opens wide in the morning, closes and dies at night. Yet the buds are so prolific that the plant seems always to be blooming and each flower's death is scarcely noticed by the casual passerby.*

These abundant buds with their curious bean-like flavor have long been an important food to the Chinese and Japanese. And, indeed, their vegetable-like quality makes them an interesting accompaniment to meat entrees or as an ingredient in one of the many exotic Oriental dishes so popular with Americans. The Chinese even have a recipe for the just-withered, end-of-day blossoms—combining these in a dish with pork tidbits and soy sauce.

If your garden does not yield an area of day lilies, keep your eye open as you travel the highways in midsummer, for day lily buds abound on wild plants everywhere.

DAY LILY DILLIES

2 pounds day lily buds
5 hot red pepper pods
5 cloves garlic
1 quart white vinegar
½ cup water
6 tablespoons salt
1 tablespoon celery seed

Wash and drain lily buds. Pack neatly in 5 hot, sterilized pint jars. Place 1 pepper pod and 1 whole garlic clove in each jar. Place remaining ingredients in a saucepan and bring to a boil. Pour over lily buds in jars and seal. Keep sealed and in a cool, dark place for 8 weeks before using. Serve cold as an appetizer with cocktails. Makes 5 pints.

SAVORY DAY LILY BUDS

1 quart of ready-to-bloom day
   lily buds
¼ teaspoon dried summer savory
¼ teaspoon salt
1 teaspoon butter

Wash and drain lily buds, removing any stems. Cover
with water in a saucepan and add salt. Bring to boil and
boil 4-5 minutes, until just tender. Drain. Crush savory
and sprinkle on buds. Add butter. Serve at once as a
vegetable accompaniment. Serves 4.

DAY LILY ROLLERS

12 thin slices cold boiled ham
1 pint fresh, young, day lily
    buds (about 36)
1 small jar prepared mustard
1 day lily blossom

Boil day lily buds as in recipe for Savory Day Lily Buds (see page 39), and drain. Place three buds in center of each ham slice which has been thinly coated with mustard. Roll up and arrange on platter. Garnish with a day lily blossom. Dried beef slices may be substituted for the ham. Serves 3-4 as a snack, or canapes.

DAY LILY TEMPURA

3 dozen semi-opened day
    lily buds
soy sauce

Prepare thin fritter batter (see Squash Blossom Fritters, page 79, and add ½ teaspoon baking powder and ¼ cup of milk to the basic batter). Wash and drain and dry lily buds. Dip each in the batter to coat all surfaces and let excess drip back into batter bowl. Lower into hot deep fat and fry until puffy and golden. Serve hot with a small bowl of soy sauce for dunking. Serves 6.

Sambucus Canadensis

ELDERFLOWERS

It's the common elderberry tree known to botanists as Sambucus canadensis *that yields its lovely clusters of white flowerettes to fritters and pancakes and crêpes.*

In England, in the merry month of May, the lacy flowerettes are plucked and dried for making a delicious and fragrant tea. The dried variety may also be used in making fritters, although only half the usual quantity is needed, since the subtle flavor is doubly strengthened by drying.

The common elder is familiar to outdoorsmen. Its delicate and lovely blossoms abound in woods wherever the climate knows a true spring.

ELDERFLOWER FLAPJACKS

2 dozen white elderflower clusters
1 quart of water
4 teaspoons salt
  pancake batter

Wash elderflowers carefully in salted water. Drain. Pluck off flower heads, removing all stems. Add 1 cup of the flowerettes to each quart of pancake batter and cook pancakes in the usual way. Serve with butter and syrup or sprinkle with sugar. One quart of batter serves 4-6.

ELDERFLOWER FRITTERS

    2 dozen white elderflower clusters
       fritter batter
       salt
       powdered sugar

Wash elderflower clusters in a quart of cold water to
which a handful of salt has been added. Remove
stems or leaves, allowing each cluster of white flowers
to remain intact. Drain on paper towels. Prepare
fritter batter (see Squash Blossom Fritters, page 79).
Dip each cluster into batter, allowing excess to drain
back into bowl. Fry in deep, hot fat until golden brown.
Sprinkle with powdered sugar and serve hot. Serves 2-4.

ELDERFLOWER MILK PUNCH

6 clusters of white elderflowers,
   washed and drained
1 quart milk
6 teaspoons honey
3 teaspoons brandy
2 teaspoons chopped fresh lemon
   balm, or
1 teaspoon grated fresh
   lemon peel
   nutmeg

Heat milk to the boiling point, but do not boil. Pour over elderflowers and lemon balm or lemon peel. Steep for 10 minutes. Strain. Add honey and brandy and cool. Serve with a sprinkling of elderflowers and a dash of nutmeg. Serves 4.

ELDERFLOWER WAFFLES

1 quart waffle batter
3 dozen white elderflower clusters

Wash clusters and remove all stems, retaining just the flowers. Toss the blossoms into the batter and gently fold in. Cook in waffle grill at once. Serve with honey or with butter and sugar. Serves 4-6.

Calendula Officinalis

MARIGOLDS

Shakespeare's "winking Mary-bud," the marigold is grown all over the world, from Africa to Mexico throughout Europe, and at all seasons in America. Not the French or African marigold common to most gardens, this is the Calendula, *sometimes nicknamed "the sun's bride."*

Its petals in dried form were used as a pot-herb long ago, and the marigold's intense color gave many a sauce and stew its golden hue. Fresh or dried, it appeared in puddings, cakes, salads, and meat dishes. And it gave its gold to certain cheeses made by the Dutch.

To dry the petals, pluck the flowers after the dew has left them in the morning. Remove the petals and lay them on foil with none overlapping. Place in a 200°F. oven for two hours or until dry enough to crumble. Store in an airtight jar until ready to use. The finely crumbled petals may be used to color rice, noodles, cream soups, and broths during cooking.

EGGS MARIGOLD

6 hard-cooked eggs
¼ cup mayonnaise
12 fresh marigolds
2 dried marigold petals
½ teaspoon salt
   pepper to taste

Peel eggs and slice in half lengthwise. Remove yolks and mash them with a fork. Add mayonnaise, salt, dried and crushed marigold petals, and pepper to taste to the yolks, blending to make a smooth paste. Refill the halved whites of eggs with yolk mixture. Remove petals from the fresh marigolds and tuck them into the centers of the stuffed eggs, arranging them so as to have a recreated flower garnishing each egg half. Chill. Serves 4-6.

MARIGOLD BREAD PUDDING

6 slices day-old white bread,
     crusts trimmed
2 eggs, lightly beaten
½ teaspoon vanilla
½ cup fresh whole milk
½ cup granulated sugar
2 tablespoons fresh marigold
     petals, chopped fine
   pinch salt
   butter

Butter a loaf pan and arrange in layers buttered slices or torn pieces of bread. Mix together eggs, vanilla, sugar, salt, milk, and marigold petals. Pour over bread. Bake at 350ºF. for 40 minutes or until a knife inserted in the center of pudding comes out clean. Serves 2-3.

Note: Raisins may be added and a light vanilla sauce served over the pudding.

MARIGOLDEN CAULIFLOWER

  1 large cauliflower
  2 teaspoons crushed, dried
      marigold petals
  1 teaspoon fresh chopped
      parsley
 ¼ cup of melted butter
  1 teaspoon salt
12 fresh marigolds

Wash and trim green leaves from cauliflower. Place in salted boiling water to cover and boil till tender, but still crisp. Do not overcook. During last 10 minutes of cooking add crushed marigold petals, being sure that cauliflower is completely immersed and becomes colored an even saffron yellow. Remove to hot plate when cooked, draining all water. Pour melted butter with chopped parsley over the cauliflower and tuck fresh marigold flowers here and there. Serves 4-6.

MARIGOLD CHEESE DIP

    1 large package cream cheese
    ½ pint sour cream
    1 teaspoon sherry
    1 teaspoon minced fresh chives
    1 teaspoon fresh summer savory,
       chopped fine
    1 tablespoon fresh marigold petals,
       chopped fine

Blend cheese, cream, and sherry until smooth. Add chives, savory, and marigold petals (if dried ones are used, soak in water for half an hour before using and drain thoroughly). Season with salt and freshly ground pepper, if desired. Refrigerate for at least one hour. Serve with chips, crackers, tacos, or on hot, small biscuits. Serves 6-12.

MARIGOLDEN CUSTARD

      3 cups milk
      4 eggs
      4 egg yolks
      ½ cup sugar
      2 drops vanilla extract
     12 fresh marigold petals, or
      6 dried marigold petals

Scald milk and remove from heat. Beat eggs and egg
yolks together with sugar until lemon-colored. Add
vanilla. Slowly add milk, stirring the egg mixture
continually. If dried marigold petals are used, crumble
them to a fine powder and stir into the custard. Butter
6 custard cups and fill. If fresh marigold petals are used,
place one or two petals in the bottom of each cup
before filling. Set cups in a pan of hot water and bake
in a 325°F. oven for 35 to 45 minutes or until a knife
inserted in the center comes out clean. Serves 6, in the
cups or unmolded on plates.

MARIGOLD RICE

3 cups instant rice
1 medium onion, sautéed
   in butter
3 cups chicken or beef bouillon
½ teaspoon rosemary
3 teaspoons dried marigold
   petals

Bring bouillon to a boil, add all other ingredients, turn off heat, and cover tightly. Allow to stand for 15 minutes. Stir with a fork and serve. Serves 6.

FISH CHOWDER MARIGOLD

1 head, tail, bones of red snapper,
    cod, fluke, flounder, hake, bass,
    or other white fish
1 small onion
1 carrot
1 bay leaf
¼ teaspoon dried thyme
3 peppercorns
1 carrot
1 teaspoon salt
1 quart water
1 tablespoon butter
1 tablespoon flour
1 quart milk
1 teaspoon dried marigold petals

Place fish bones and head in large pot with water to cover. Add peeled and sliced onion and carrot, bay leaf, thyme, peppercorns, salt. Bring to boil and simmer for 45 minutes or until flesh falls from fish heads. Remove all bones from the liquid, leaving all other ingredients. Cool. Whirl in blender and reserve. Make a roux or white sauce by melting butter in soup pot and blending flour. Add milk a little at a time, letting sauce thicken. Add marigold petals and additional salt and freshly ground pepper to taste. Add blender contents. Stir and turn up to high heat. Add additional milk. Heat again. Serves 6.

Note: Diced cooked potatoes may be added to thicken. A jiffy version: add marigold petals to two cans of fish chowder and prepare according to directions on can.

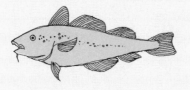

Trapaeolum Majus

NASTURTIUMS

A native of Peru, the nasturtium offers not only its brilliant flowers but its stems, leaves and little green seeds to the gourmet's table. Nearly a hundred varieties of this tender plant exist and a child can cultivate it as easily as radishes or scallions.

Nicknamed "Indian Cress," the nasturtium is a member of the cress family and its young, pale green leaves are evocative of the flavor of watercress, although more delicate and somewhat less peppery. The young leaves and stems are delightful in salads, alone, or tossed with other tender greens such as field salad or Bibb lettuce.

Its blossoms in brilliant shades of red, orange and yellow are delicious in salads and sandwich spreads and serve as beautiful garnishes for salads and hors d'oeuvres. The berry-like green seed buds that appear after the plant has blossomed are an elegant substitute for capers, an adjunct to pickling spices and marinades.

NASTURTIUM ASPIC

1 package lemon-flavored gelatin
1 cup finely shredded green cabbage
1 dozen nasturtium blossoms

Pinch out stamens (centers) of washed nasturtium blossoms and reserve blossoms. Prepare gelatin according to package directions and refrigerate until cooled to a thick thick, sirupy stage. Rinse a one-quart ring mold in cold water and pour in gelatin to a depth of ½ inch. Chill until firm. Arrange blossoms face down on the layer of chilled gelatin. Pour enough gelatin over to cover and chill till firm. Add shredded cabbage and pour remaining gelatin into mold. Chill till firm. Unmold and garnish with additional nasturtium blossoms and/or leaves. Serves 4 to 6.

NASTURTIUM CONSOMME

2 cans clear consommé
2 dozen nasturtium blossoms
6 nasturtium leaves

Wash and drain nasturtium blossoms and leaves. Reserve leaves and six blossoms, placing in refrigerator or ice water to crisp. Heat consommé. Finely chop remaining blossoms. Just before serving, stir chopped blossoms into consommé and garnish each serving with a single blossom floated on a stemless leaf. Serves 6.

NASTURTIUM FLOWER RICE

1 cup of instant rice
1 cup of canned consommé
2 dozen nasturtium blossoms

Remove green base and inside (stamens and pistils) from blossoms. Wash and drain and chop fine. Put rice and consommé in a saucepan and bring to a boil. Add the chopped blossoms, cover tightly and turn off heat. The piquant yellow rice will be ready to serve in 10 minutes. Serves 3-4.

NASTURTIUM MAYONNAISE

½ pint good mayonnaise
2 dozen nasturtium blossoms
2 tablespoons heavy cream

Depending on the intensity of the color of the blossoms used, this makes a decorative dressing for hearts of lettuce, sliced tomatoes, cucumber salad, or avocado stuffed with crabmeat. Simply place all ingredients in an electric blender and whirl at high speed for one minute. Place in jar and store in refrigerator until ready for use. Makes slightly more than ½ pint of dressing.

NASTURTIUM NIBBLES

3 dozen nasturtium blossoms
1 small jar cream cheese with chives
1 small jar pineapple cream cheese
1 small jar or can of ham salad spread

Wash, drain and set aside blossoms. Allow cheese spreads and ham salad to soften at room temperature. Carefully stuff each blossom with a small amount of one of the spreads. Arrange on a serving tray and chill. Serve as a cocktail hors d'oeuvre. Serves 6-8. Other stuffings that are suited to this attractive dish are: fresh crabmeat salad, egg salad, tuna fish salad, salmon salad, red caviar mixed with softened cream cheese, or clam dip.

NASTURTIUM SALAD

1 head of Boston lettuce
or
2 heads of Bibb lettuce
3 hard-cooked eggs
3 dozen nasturtium leaves
8 nasturtium blossoms
½ teaspoon salt
   pepper
3 teaspoons peanut oil
1 teaspoon vinegar

Pull apart and tear lettuce into bite-size pieces. Place in lettuce basket with nasturtium leaves and wash thoroughly. Drain. Place salt, oil, vinegar and pepper to taste (one or two full turns of the pepper grinder) in bottom of salad bowl and mix. Add greens and quartered hard-cooked eggs. Toss until thoroughly coated with dressing. Garnish with whole nasturtium flowers. Serves 4.

NASTURTIUM SANDWICHES

8 thin slices of whole-wheat or
   white bread
½ stick sweet butter
2 dozen large nasturtium blossoms

Wash and drain blossoms and place in refrigerator to crisp for an hour. Trim crusts from the thinly sliced bread and spread each with unsalted butter. Chop all but four nasturtium blossoms until finely minced. Sprinkle each buttered slice of bread with blossoms and put together to make four sandwiches. Garnish each with a whole blossom. An alternate way: Soften butter and blend with blossoms to spread on bread slices. Or substitute cream cheese for butter as a variation. Makes four whole sandwiches or eight halves.

NASTURTIUM VINEGAR

1 pint jar of nasturtium blossoms
1 pint of wine or cider vinegar

Use a wide-mouthed pint jar that can be securely sealed. Fill with nasturtium blossoms and pour vinegar over them to cover. Seal. Store in refrigerator or cool place for four weeks. Open and check flavor. If more intense flavor is desired, reseal and store for two to three weeks longer. Then strain and rebottle. Use in vinegar and oil dressings for tossed green salads or for nasturtium leaf salads. Makes 1 pint.

Rosa

ROSES

A symbol of love, the true flower of Venus, loveliest to look upon in all its shapes and colors, sweetest to smell in its myriad fragrances, the rose has been an ingredient of delicacies for the table since the beginnings of civilized man.

Rich in vitamin C, its syrup was a staple of medieval pharmacies, and today, rose hips are said to have 400 times more vitamin C than orange juice. The lovely fragrance of the blossoms still enhances jams and jellies and honeys which tantalize the tongue and the nose when spread on warm, fresh bread, or hot biscuits.

It is the old-fashioned varieties, including the wild rose, which best yield their petals to the recipes that follow. Present day hybrids with strong, tough stems and glorious nuances of color have tougher petals, less fragrance than the earlier, simpler species.

So, if you can, pluck your petals from a Cabbage, Damask, Moss, Rugosa, or other old-fashioned rosebush. Use the modern roses to please the eye — in decorating birthday cakes or to float in festive punches and finger bowls.

CRYSTALLIZED ROSE PETALS

1   pint fresh red rose petals
1   egg white, slightly beaten
1   cup fine granulated white sugar

Wash, drain and dry rose petals. Dip each first in the egg white (a little red food coloring may be added if desired), then in the sugar, being sure to coat all surfaces completely. Place on ungreased cookie sheets and dry in the sun or in a very slow oven (250°F.) until firm and crystallized. Place in tin container between layers of waxed paper, seal tightly and keep in a cool, dry place until ready to use. These are lovely as garnishes for cakes, puddings, ice cream desserts, or served simply as an after-dinner confection.

ROSE BOWL

    1 cup rose syrup
    1 quart of club soda
    1 bottle of rosé wine
    2 dozen Moss roses
    2 limes sliced wafer-thin

Place roses in ice-cube trays — one rose per cube — add water and freeze. When ready to serve, pour syrup (see Rose Cooler recipe, page 71), soda, and wine over cubes in punch bowl. Float lime slices on top. Serves 8 to 12.

ROSE BUTTER

1 quart fresh rose petals
1 pound butter
½ cup salt

Spread rose petals on ungreased cookie sheets and dry in a slow (250°F.) oven. When thoroughly dry, place in a deep casserole in layers, sprinkling each layer liberally with salt. Place butter on top. Cover casserole securely and allow butter to remain thus for two to three days while it absorbs the rose petal fragrance and flavor. Use this butter to spread on toast, hot biscuits or warm bread.

ROSE COOLER

1 quart fresh red rose petals,
      packed tightly
1 pint water
2 cups sugar
8 whole cloves

Put all ingredients into a saucepan with a tight lid. Bring to a boil. Reduce heat and simmer gently with lid on for 45 minutes to 1 hour. When cool, strain into sterilized bottle and store in refrigerator until ready to use. Make a cooler by adding 2 jiggers of this rose syrup to a tumbler of soda water. It is also delightful in iced tea.

ROSE ICE CREAM

1 pint vanilla ice cream
½ cup crimson rose petals
2 tablespoons superfine sugar
½ cup rosé wine
12 crystallized red rose petals

Put washed rose petals (snip off the white bases), sugar and wine in blender and whirl for one minute. Soften the ice cream and mix with contents of blender. Pour in freezing tray and refreeze overnight, stirring once or twice. Serve in sherbet glasses with crystallized rose petals for garnish. Serves 4.

ROSE PETAL SALAD

1 pint fresh rose petals,
   loosely packed
1 head of chicory
1 head of Boston lettuce
   rose vinegar
   peanut oil
   salt
   pepper

Pull apart, wash and drain lettuce and chicory. Crisp in refrigerator. Wash and dry rose petals. Mix in preferred proportions a vinegar-oil dressing (see recipe for Rose (Vinegar, page 74), adding salt and pepper to taste. Tear chicory and lettuce into bite-size pieces. Put greens and petals in large salad bowl. Sprinkle with dressing and toss until completely coated. Serves 6-8.

ROSE VINEGAR

1 cup fresh rose petals, tightly
    packed
1 pint white wine vinegar

Place washed and drained rose petals in a quart jar with
a rubber-ring screw top. Pour vinegar over petals. Seal
jar tightly and place in a sunny window for 2-3 weeks.
Open jar, strain contents through hair sieve or a large
coffee filter paper. Put strained vinegar in stoppered
cruet. Use for all kinds of tossed green salads, especially
for Rose Petal Salad (page 73). Makes 1 pint.

WILD ROSE JELLY

2½ cups canned apple juice
1 quart fresh wild rose petals,
    tightly packed
3¾ cups granulated sugar
½ bottle Certo
    red food coloring or carmine
    paraffin

Heat apple juice to the boiling point but do not boil.
Place washed and drained rose petals in large saucepan
and pour hot apple juice over them. Bring to boil and
boil 20 minutes. Strain off juice into another large
saucepan. Add sugar, stir. Add two drops of carmine
(available at pharmacy) or red vegetable coloring to tint
juice a rose color. Bring to boil, stirring. Add Certo. Boil
for 1 more minute. Pour at once into sterilized jelly glasses and cover with melted paraffin immediately.
Makes 6 standard jelly glasses full.

Cucurbita Pepo

SQUASH FLOWERS

Perhaps the most native of all vegetables to the United
States is the squash. It is truly a food from antiquity, for
its seeds and rind have been found in dried state in ruins
dating as far back as 2000 B.C. The Italians, however,
have explored and exploited this delicacy to include the
use of its flowers as an edible. Indeed, in the early spring
in Italian markets, one of the most prized foods is the
bud of the vivid orange blossom—with its delicate and
elusive squash-like flavor.

On the following pages, you will find several recipes for
surprisingly delectable dishes made with this young
flower. Our own zucchini, summer squash, and the well-
known early yellow variety all yield buds that provide
this unusually delicious ingredient for dishes to add to
spring and summer menus.

SAUTEED SQUASH FLOWERS

1 pint squash flower buds, partially
   opened
2 tablespoons olive oil or butter
½ teaspoon salt
   pepper

Since the preparation of this dish is dramatic, it is enter-
taining for guests to make it at the table. A crêpes pan
may be used, or an electric skillet, if desired. Heat oil or
butter in the pan. Add washed and dried squash flower
buds and turn them for a few minutes. Most will burst
into blossom as they cook. Do not brown. Sprinkle with
salt and freshly ground pepper. Serve at once as a vegetable accompaniment to fish or meat course. Serves 4.

SQUASH BLOSSOM FRITTERS

1 quart squash blossoms
1 cup flour
½ teaspoon salt
2 eggs
1¼ cup milk
1 teaspoon melted butter

Choose blossoms which have opened about half way. Wash, drain and pat dry. Sift flour and salt together. Beat eggs until lemon-colored and fluffy. Add milk and melted butter to eggs. Mix. Add flour gradually, stirring to prevent lumps from forming. Meanwhile, heat deep fat to 370°F. Dip each blossom in batter to coat, and fry until golden brown. Drain on paper towels and keep hot in warming oven until all are fried. Serve as is or with a sprinkling of salt. Serves 4-6.

SQUASH FLOWER SCRAMBLE

4 eggs
1 dozen squash blossoms
2 tablespoons milk
¼ teaspoon salt
   pepper

Beat eggs, milk, salt and pepper to taste with a wire whisk until frothy. Reserve 4 of the prettiest blossoms. Remove sepals, stamens and any green from remaining blossoms and chop finely. Add to eggs and turn into skillet with melted butter. Cook and scramble to desired degree of doneness. Serve with squash flowers as garnish. Serves 2.

STUFFED SQUASH FLOWERS

½ pound ground chuck beef
1 cup cooked rice
½ teaspoon dried oregano
½ teaspoon salt
¼ teaspoon freshly ground black
   pepper
1 teaspoon instant minced onion
1 egg
1 dozen large squash flowers

Place squash flowers in ice water to crisp. Mix remaining ingredients together. Drain flowers and stuff each with the rice-meat mixture, folding ends of flowers over to form neat, small packets. Butter a casserole and lay the flower packets close together on the bottom. Pour a cup of instant bouillon over all. Dot with butter. Bake for about 20 minutes at 350°F. Serves 4.

Viola Odorata

VIOLETS

The violet is a feast for the eye as well as the palate. A member of the herb family, the appealing blossom, as well as its leaves, can be eaten in many delicious ways.

As a confection, the blossom vies with the rose when it is sugar-frosted or candied. As a fresh-blossom garnish for tea sandwiches, salads, festive cakes or cookies, it knows no rival.

Some 600 violet species exist in both wild and cultivated states. Some are fragrant, although most are odorless. Colors range from pure white to various shades of yellow, pink and lavender or purple.

For the recipes contained here, the common wild purple species Viola odorata, the Sweet Violet, found in the woods in the spring, serves best, looks most decorative, and tastes and smells sweetest.

CANDIED VIOLETS

1 large bouquet of violets
2 egg whites
1 cup fine granulated sugar
¼ teaspoon extract of violet
   (optional)
   waxed paper

Wash and drain flowers. Remove stems and all green, but keep flower petals intact and joined. Be sure flowers are thoroughly dry and, if necessary, gently blot between absorbent paper towels. Beat egg whites until white and foamy, but not stiff. Dip each flower in egg white (to which you may add a drop or two of purple food coloring if desired), coating on all sides; then dip and coat thoroughly in sugar. Place on waxed paper and open petals with toothpick so that none are stuck together. Keep flowers separated on the paper and dry in the sun or in a warm, dry place. Store in an airtight tin or jar. Use as a garnish or eat as candy. If a violet flavor is desired, add extract (available at drug stores) to egg white while beating. These ingredients will make approximately 6 dozen.

VIOLET BOMBE

1 pint vanilla ice cream
½ pint heavy whipping cream
4 dozen crystallized or candied violets

Whip cream until it stands in peaks and "molds." Scoop ice cream with round scoop into four sherbet glasses, putting it flat side down. Put whipped cream into pastry tube with rosette tip and cover each scoop of ice cream with rosettes placed closely together. Work quickly. Center each rosette with a candied violet (see recipe on page 84). Serves 4.

VIOLET OMELET

  4 eggs
  4 teaspoons milk
12 violet leaves
12 violet blossoms
     salt
     pepper
  1 teaspoon butter

Wash violet leaves and blossoms and crisp in refrigerator. Beat eggs with fork or whisk until light yellow. Add milk. Sprinkle with salt and add freshly ground pepper (about three turns of the grinder). Melt butter in skillet. Pour egg mixture in and, using spatula, cut around edges of pan and across egg mixture until top of mixture is frothy and bubbly. Meanwhile chop violet leaves and sprinkle on top of egg mixture. Turn omelet by folding over and cook further until desired degree of doneness. Serve on hot plate. Sprinkle or garnish with violet blossoms. Serves 2.

VIOLET SALAD

3 dozen violet blossoms
1 bunch watercress
1 head Iceberg lettuce
1 teaspoon vinegar
3 teaspoons peanut oil
  salt
  pepper

Wash violet blossoms and remove stems and all green sepals, but leave petals and flowers intact. Wash watercress and lettuce and shake till dry. Tear lettuce into small pieces. In bottom of salad bowl, mix vinegar with oil, add salt and freshly ground pepper to taste and mix thoroughly. Add watercress and lettuce; toss and turn until all leaves are coated with dressing. Add violet blossoms, and turn two or three times. Serves 6.

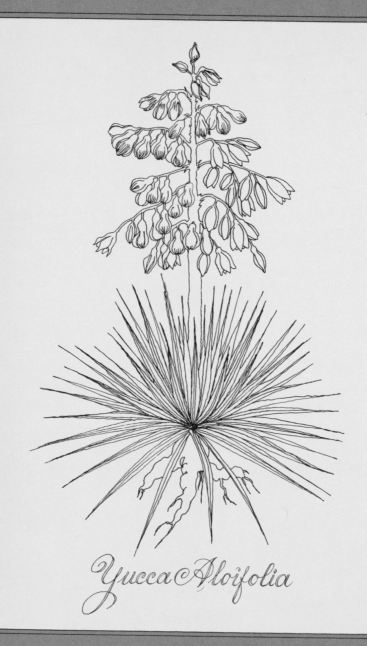

Yucca Aloifolia

YUCCA

The ubiquitous yucca, a spiky evergreen plant, sends its creamy, ghostly spire of blooms skyward around the world. Its tough, straplike, pointed leaves — sharp as swords — have given one variety the name Spanish Bayonet or Spanish Dagger. This species, Yucca aloifolia, *bears hundreds of blossoms varying in size from two to three inches long, and in southern United States, Mexico, the West Indies, and throughout South America, the blossoms are considered a great delicacy.*

Used in soups, salads, and with eggs, yucca flowers have a cool, aromatic flavor. The plant also bears a fruit which is eaten by Southern Indian families much in the manner of bananas. In Guatamela, the creamy white flowers of the Spanish Bayonet are sold in the markets and called "Flor de Izote." Boiled or fried, the petals evoke the flavor of fresh asparagus.

FLOR DE IZOTE SOUP

3 cups fresh, washed yucca
   petals
2 large fresh tomatoes, peeled
1 fresh green pepper, diced
1 large onion, sliced thin
1 teaspoon fresh basil, minced
1 clove garlic, minced
1 pint water
¼ teaspoon freshly ground pepper
1 tablespoon sugar
½ teaspoon salt
1 package frozen peas

Put all ingredients except peas in soup pot and cook slowly for one hour. Taste, add additional salt, if desired; add frozen peas. Cook 15 minutes more. Serves 4.

FLUFFY YUCCA OMELETS

1 cup yucca petals, lightly
    packed
6 eggs
¼ teaspoon freshly ground pepper
½ teaspoon salt
    paprika for garnish

Cook petals in boiling water with salt and pepper for about 10 minutes. Drain thoroughly. Allow two eggs per individual omelet. Separate yolks from whites and beat separately. Yolks should be a lemon color and whites fluffy but not stiff. Fold yolks and whites together; add one third of the yucca petals to each two-egg omelet and fry lightly in butter until golden brown and puffy. Sprinkle with paprika; add additional salt and pepper to taste. Serves 3.

YUCCA BLOSSOM-HEART SALAD

1 cup yucca blossom hearts
1 head lettuce
½ cup Italian or French
dressing

Remove centers or "hearts" of yucca blossoms and wash in cold water. (Reserve petals for another dish.) Boil for about 10 minutes in lightly salted water. Drain. Cool. Marinate one hour in the salad dressing. Drain marinade and serve chilled on lettuce leaves. Serves 2 to 4.

YUCCA FLOWER SALAD

1 quart yucca petals, not packed
3 tablespoons peanut oil
1 tablespoon white vinegar
½ teaspoon salt
⅛ teaspoon freshly ground pepper
1 pinch chervil, optional

Pluck blossoms early in the morning. Remove centers, reserving only the petals. Wash, drain in salad basket, and place in crisper to chill in refrigerator for an hour or two. Blend remaining ingredients in salad bowl. Just before serving, toss petals in the dressing. If desired, reserve a few flower centers, chop fine, and sprinkle over the salads. (The flavor is a slightly bitter one.) Serves 6.